HEARTLAND

HEARTLAND

Prairie Portraits & Landscapes

Photographs by Ottmar Bierwagen

Text by Mark Abley

Douglas & McIntyre

Vancouver/Toronto

89 90 91 92 93   5 4 3 2 1

Douglas & McIntyre Ltd.
1615 Venables Street
Vancouver, British Columbia   V5L 2H1

Canadian Cataloguing in Publication Data

Bierwagen, Ottmar.
  Heartland

  ISBN 0-88894-656-2

  1. Prairie Provinces - Description and travel -
1981–   - Views.* I. Abley, Mark, 1955–   II. Title.
FC3243.2.B53 1989   971.2′03′0222   C89-091306-4
F1060.92.B53 1989

Design by Fiona MacGregor
Typeset by The Typeworks
Printed and bound in Singapore by C.S. Graphics Pte. Ltd.

To the people of the prairies, with special thanks to Doyle and Karen Mullaney,
whose friendship and western hospitality will always be remembered.

Ottmar Bierwagen

In memory of Caroline Heath

Mark Abley

Y ou step into your car, and you drive out of town. It doesn't matter where—just out. The suburbs give way to a mile of neon enticement. And when the last house, the last gas station or motel or fast-food franchise has fallen out of sight in your rear-view mirror, the sky all around you opens up. Above a barn off to the left, a dark hawk is turning its heavy wings. You grow aware of cloud formations, of the different weathers stirring over several edges of the horizon. The dry light of the west hurts your eyes and, at the same time, sharpens their sense of colour, transforming a simple warning sign into a yellow diamond by the road. Then the car speeds past, or a cloud impedes the sun, and the diamond is gone.

Soon your breathing slows down. After a few minutes at the wheel, you find the moods and rhythms of the city alien, a trifle absurd. As you think back on them, shaking your head, a neck muscle starts to uncoil. The striped highway stretches far in front of you, never curving, reaching its vanishing point at a low, remote hill. The road resembles (you suddenly realize) a delicate yet powerful bone, a taut spine that divides the massive fields on either side. You have a sense of passing over the skin of some drowsy animal, of skimming the flanks of a living creature whose body is as big as the sky.

You turn off the highway onto a gravel road, then pull the car to a stop and open a door to meet the rush of air. No matter where you're coming from, it's hard to escape the prairie wind. Your ears ache as you lean on the car's roof and watch the rolling world. People have gone crazy out here trying to understand exactly what the wind is saying. It's no use, it doesn't speak any of our languages.

Back in the driver's seat, you ride a cloud of yellow-brown dust in the direction of the nearest town. You know where it lies by the telltale silhouette of grain elevators breaking the horizon, but you're a little surprised at how long it takes you to arrive—even from afar, the intense clarity of the atmosphere makes the town appear close at hand. Along the roadside, barbed-wire fences are heaped with tumbleweed, as though in silent parody of an Old World hedgerow. Most of the sloughs are now bare earth, caked by an alkali salt, and there's no sign of wild ducks. It's hard to recall the last good rain. You pass farms where brightly painted machinery waits in the big yard, ready for use. You pass other farms, too, where the paint on the forsaken buildings has eroded everywhere but the underside of a sturdy roof;

collapsed, thistle-ridden farms, where the wind and a passing car provide the only noise. In what used to be a garden, derelict machines are returning to the earth.

Only a handful of people are about when you ease the car over the railway lines, make a sharp left and a right, and join the dozen other vehicles parked on Main Street. At first sight, the wooden buildings look flimsy and disappointing. They would need to be four or five times higher to do justice to the street's great width. You get out of the car and prowl the sidewalks for a couple of minutes, feeling conspicuous. The residents, it seems, have some makeshift business arrangements: for two days of the week, a medical clinic occupies part of the firehall, and the TV and video store also sells ice cream. Pinned on a civic noticeboard, alongside posters for bingo games and bowling parties and a Lutheran bake sale next Saturday afternoon, a baleful sheet spells out "Jehovah's Warnings to Christendom". Across the street are a placid, white-painted church, an immobile half-ton truck and a black dog running.

You walk to the town's hotel: eight little-used rooms and a bar. A long, air-conditioned room with no windows and a low ceiling, the bar seems to take some kind of perverse pride in shutting out the light that washes the rest of town. A handwritten sign at the front of the bar—"There's No Beer In Hell So Y Not Drink It Here"—overlooks tables where you can try your hand at pool and miniature hockey. In addition to a Brown Cow, Blue Lagoon or Black Russian, you could order a Pioneer Bliss: ten ounces of Alberta vodka in a pitcher of lime juice. You ask for a beer instead. The waitress is bored and wants to talk about the city: it's where her younger brother lives, and where she'd like to move herself. One day, she'll have enough money. She draws hard on a cigarette. Is it true what they say about that new shopping mall?

The beer gives you an appetite, but you don't feel like risking your luck at the Sincere Restaurant on the other side of the street. For a few moments, a passing tractor hides the restaurant's metal sign: two hands shaking. A speck of hard dust, probably a gift from the tractor, makes your right eye water. There ought to be a Chinese restaurant here; every prairie town used to have one. But where? You pass Rose's empty Beauty Parlor and a hardware store and the Co-op, where you stop to read another noticeboard. This town is full of messages. The board carries news of three upcoming auction sales, at which every kind of commodity from horse collars to microwave ovens, pipe racks to pendulum clocks, ice-cream churns to barber chairs and a set of Depression-glass salt and pepper shakers will be sold to the highest bidder. Perhaps the sellers accumulated this bric-a-brac at earlier farm auctions. You don't lug a barber chair to a new subdivision of Calgary; you don't need a horse collar to grace your golden years in Victoria.

Here's the Chinese restaurant, around the corner from the three grain elevators. And inside, here's a good cross-section of the townspeople. You settle onto a spotless red chair, facing the window, and examine the menu. It promises a choice of Canadian-style Chinese food—egg rolls, chop suey, chow mein—or such un-Chinese delicacies as bacon billie and cherry pie. Everybody else sits in booths around the sides of the room, keeping a good eye on you. There's a blond family of five below a Credit Union calendar; there's a couple of teenage girls chewing gum near a ceramic statue of a fat Chinaman. A painting of a Rocky Mountain sunset is framed by wood and also by two red strips of paper down the side, each strip containing a half-dozen Chinese characters. The painting hangs above an old man and an old woman, both eating hot pork sandwiches flooded in gravy.

They sit kitty-corner from each other, at opposite edges of the table. He's kept his peaked cap on, the one with the inscription that reads: FARM FRESH. Her tight, supervised hair suggests a recent visit to Rose's. They're not saying a word to each other, not while the good food lasts. But elsewhere in the restaurant, people are talking . . .

14

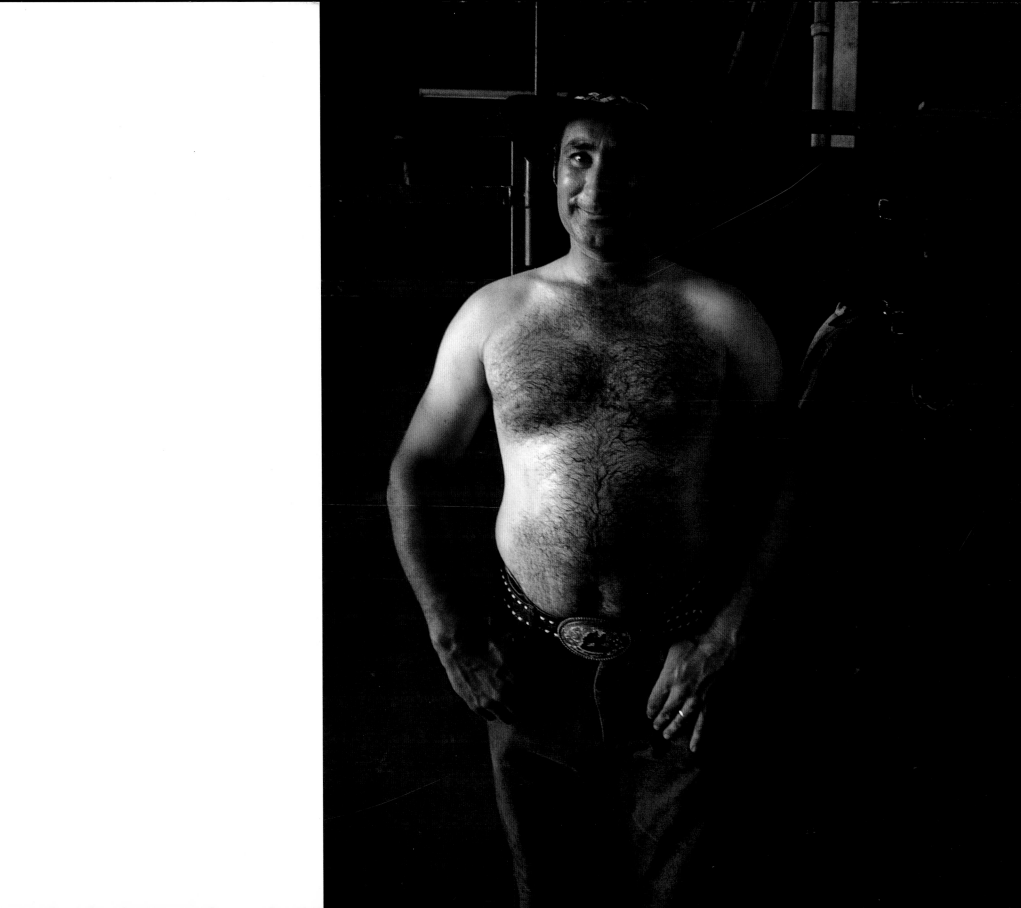

22

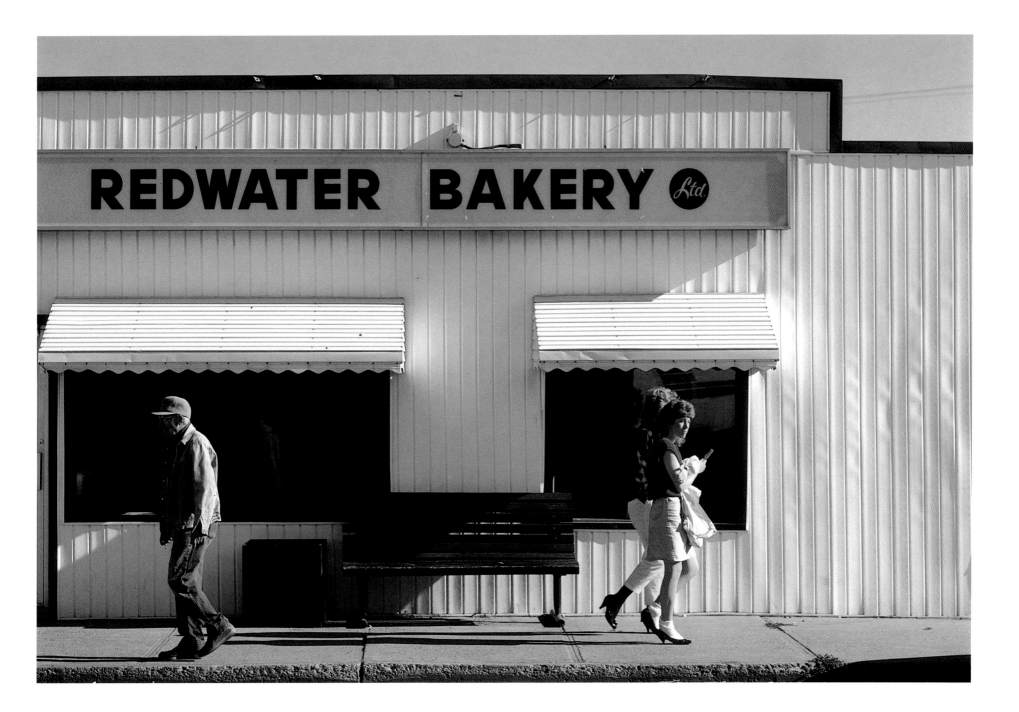

Prior to the white man's takeover of the Canadian prairies, a good number of explorers, traders, geographers and more or less eccentric travellers made their way through the region and recorded their impressions. Those impressions were generally of awe, of astonishment, of latent potential. The Frenchman Gabriel Franchère, who journeyed from west to east across the continent in 1814, was dumbfounded by the beauty of the Saskatchewan River: "The banks are perfectly charming, and offer in many places the fairest, the most smiling, and the most diversified scene that can be imagined." Nine years later, a young American naturalist named W. H. Keating contemplated "the broad expanse of verdant prairie, spreading beyond the utmost extent of vision," in the Red River country of what is nowadays southern Manitoba. Keating was the first to remark on a common prairie experience: "an optical illusion that makes the traveller fancy himself in the centre of a basin, and surrounded by an amphitheatre of rising ground at no great distance, which constantly eludes his approach." It's not only that the west looks different to an outsider (Keating hailed from near the Atlantic seaboard); it's also that in order to see clearly, the outsider has to look differently at the west. Eastern notions of perspective, scale and beauty no longer apply. Eastern light, after all, is tinged with mist.

Franchère, Keating and most of their fellow travellers were optimistic about the chances for permanent settlement in the region. Few of them stopped to consider that the plains, parkland, foothills and forest were already the home of many Indian nations. But the most thorough and painstaking of those early expeditions into the unmapped territory of the northwest sounded a warning note that has never been entirely silenced. Captain John Palliser's team, which explored the west between 1857 and 1860, described a big, triangular, "more or less arid desert" stretching from the United States border all the way up to the 52nd Parallel. It was an area, Palliser thought, where settlement would be unwise.

A couple of generations later, the prairies were thrown open to homesteaders. For a time the Palliser Triangle was derided, its very existence denied. "I am The Great ALBERTA," proclaims a boostering poster issued in 1910: "The Empire of Fulfillment. The land where opportunities are unlimited and the climate ideal. I am prosperity to him who would enter my gates."

In some cases, the promise held true. In some cases it still holds true. Apart from the uncertain wealth deriving from oil and gas, tourism and cattle, there is land in the north of the province even now being opened up for farming. If the greenhouse effect takes hold, farms may be created on land we think of as perpetual forest. But the first wave of settlers often found no fulfilment. Throughout much of the Palliser Triangle, the climate and soil are scarcely ideal for farming, and the opportunities for any kind of success have proven to be negligible. The vast majority of immigrants who tried their luck in southeastern Alberta were forced to move elsewhere even before the onset of the Great Depression. Since then, the area has become a wilderness of unpopulated, sage-scented rangeland interspersed with dry lakebeds, a handful of working ranches and the occasional oil rig. Most of the region's communities are now ghost towns, or have disappeared into the wind. A few, such as Etzikom and Manyberries, hang onto a fragile existence.

The brief history and desolate landscape of southeastern Alberta stand as warnings, even for parts of the rural west that are normally wet enough to nourish wheat. In the 1980s, a drought ravaged farmland far beyond the traditional confines of the Palliser Triangle and hard times returned to much of the region. The long crisis left men and women feeling resentful at their own powerlessness. All their practical intelligence, all their physical strength, all their intimacy with prices and forecasts and machines, counted for nothing in the face of the their exploits; by contrast, Louis Riel, Sitting Bull and the young heroes of the North West Mounted Police stared into a camera for posterity. As a result, perhaps, we tend to see the region's history as a disconnected series of visual images. The camera has enormous power as a means of capturing our life, and we may even look at the actual prairie as though it were a photograph. A plane once carried me over eastern Saskatchewan in the first week of November, when the harvested earth looked sombre but the frozen lakes and sloughs were white; the patchwork effect struck me as a giant black-and-white negative of a slowly unfolding picture. The aircraft's rectangular windows acted as a perfect frame. I didn't have a camera with me, yet I experienced the world as a photographic image.

No matter what the angle of vision, the prairie landscape defies a human sense of scale. It's too boundless, too awe-provoking for the imagination to contain. There's nothing comfortable about it, let alone comforting. It is, nevertheless, one of the most altered environments on the planet. Canada's largest remaining expanse of original tallgrass prairie is a sad patch of a few acres inside Winnipeg's city limits. Even where the land is devoid of towns and farms, the hands of the dead remain evident. Cattle, tumbleweed and wheat are immigrants to the west just as much as blue jeans, beer and the English language. In the places where the kingdom of wheat is faltering, tumbledown buildings and ruined machines offer tangible proof of an attempt to master nature.

Yet no one who knows them thinks of the prairies as a mastered land. Most of the men and women who belong there feel a sense of powerlessness at times, but the power of sky and distance, earth and light and weather, remains constant, implacable. One of the tasks of any landscape artist in the west is to convey this sheer strength of nature. Charles Jefferys, who was among the first painters to portray the region with faithfulness and vitality, once commented in a notebook: "Prairie like panther, tawny, indolent, fierce, lithe, feline, grace of line." An excellent figure of speech, yet—like every other figure of speech—ultimately inadequate. The prairie defeats language. There's nothing catlike about it on certain brutal days.

To see the inadequacy of most landscape pictures of the west, take a look at one of those commercial calendars that purport to show the nation's scenic beauty. The western photographs in them are so hackneyed, so boring and predictable, that it seems entirely appropriate the French word *cliché* should also mean a photographic negative. Maybe the calendar-makers return, year after year, to waving wheat fields and towering grain elevators because the buyers of calendars enjoy a sense of familiarity—no matter how meagrely those pictures convey the true and complex beauty of the west. Such photographs respond to neither of two alternative, equally compelling ways of seeing the western landscape: on the one hand, the richly detailed; on the other, the abstracting. The prairies often lend themselves to abstraction—think of the geometric patterns made by roads, big fields and the endlessly receding horizon; or contemplate the sudden, dramatic impact of a vertical object (a fencepost, a telephone pole, a stray tree) in a horizontal world.

Some of Ottmar Bierwagen's photographs of the prairies and foothills have this abstracting quality, like a quick sketch of a mile of life in the eye of God. But equally often, his work attends to the abundance of small details that bring a scene alive. The magnificent sky is not only high overhead, it also shines in the eyes and faces of Bierwagen's subjects. In his wry shots of small towns, he catches both the desperate humour and the underlying impulse towards dignity. He also takes landscape photographs in which the borders of each image seem apt. A mediocre snapshot of a field, ranch or valley can leave the viewer puzzled as to why the photographer should have chosen these arbitrary bounds. On the prairies, nature abhors a frame even more than a vacuum. That's why the view from a car window is always a distortion.

Bierwagen took these pictures in the present tense; then the moment passed. All of them, even the apparently timeless ones, are the record of time past. Would a photograph of the future have the same appeal to us, or carry the same moral weight?

46

48

54

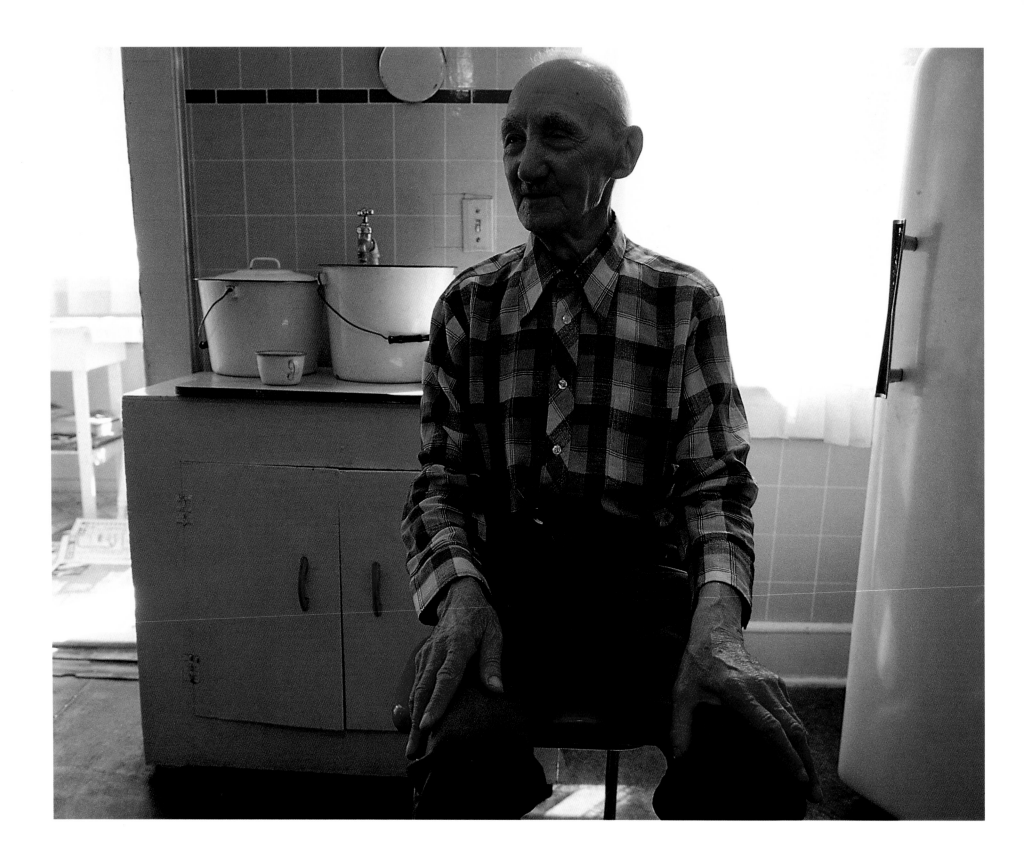

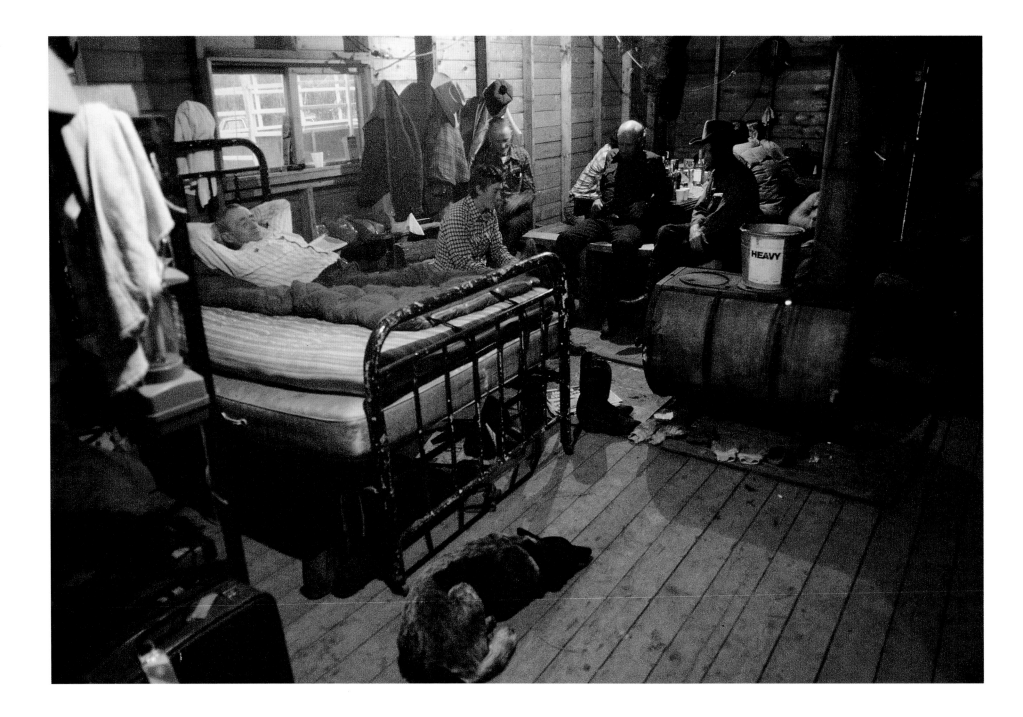

66

There are many ways to read an image. "Read" is a figure of speech, of course; it's equally possible to say there are many ways to listen to an image. What follows is a single reading of a single photograph. Other readings of the same picture are to be encouraged.

The sun is beginning to set over a city called Lethbridge. Retaining the afternoon's heat, the southern Alberta air is stained by a fine dust. Not much rain falls on this part of the world; farmers in the district irrigate or go bust. Loose, powdery topsoil gives a smoky tinge to the light. It's a fine evening for baseball, for barbecues, for romance.

A century ago, this place was named Coal Banks. It was a mining town nestled in the wide valley of the Oldman River. Then it moved up onto the plain, acquired a new name, and grew both eastward and genteel. A high black bridge, with a structure as intricate as human limbs, was built to carry coal, grain, sugar beets and other commodities towards the hungry Pacific. Below it, the valley remained half wild: a place for illicit adult encounters as well as a hunting ground for boys from town who were not frightened of ghosts or rattlesnakes. In the nineteenth century the valley had been the site of a notorious whiskey fort, now demolished. It was the site, too, of a terrible battle in which, faced by the irredeemable loss of land and culture and buffalo, thousands of Cree and Blackfoot men turned their despairing fury on each other.

An Indian man is climbing out of the valley where so many of his ancestors left this world behind in a pool of blood or a haze of alcohol. Young, long-limbed, with a shock of black hair, he's taller than they would have been. If he'd been around before the whiskey dealers, mounted police, miners, cowboys, traders, farmers, preachers, prostitutes and government agents found their way here from the south and east, he might have made a fearsome warrior. If, if, if. . . . These days, many native men never have the chance to work out a good destiny for themselves. The society of mainstream Canada prefers to forget all about them, though it still makes an uneasy profit from their thirst. Up the hill, behind the photographer's back, stands a large brewery.

A freight train is heading into Lethbridge, its front lights blazing. Crossing the tall bridge, the driver suffers the illusion of being suspended in air; the curling river far below him is almost lost in cottonwoods and shrubbery. A sweet-smelling breeze keeps the driver cool and mindful of his work. If he looks over his shoulder and shields his eyes, he can see the Rocky Mountains where the Oldman River begins.

The bridge beneath his many wheels once symbolized the achievements, the potential, the pride of the young city. For a long time after Europeans, Americans and eastern Canadians had occupied the Indian and Metis land of the west, railways served as lifelines; no community could hope to develop away from the tracks. The architecture, the shape, the physical and emotional rituals of thousands of towns across the prairies all bear the mark of railways. Even today, many people who left the west as adults find themselves irresistibly moved by the long, grieving whistle of a faraway train. But in the last few decades, the railway has lost some of its old magic and most of its old power. About 2,500 miles of prairie branch lines have been torn up in the past ten years; passenger trains are nearly extinct; even the subtle mysteries of freight rates no longer dominate the economic discussions of western cabinets. History is fast and merciless here: we have new national dreams, new spikes to drive.

Outside the city, the young Indian is making his solitary way up a paved road. He keeps his back to the bridge. For a moment, he looks as still as the nearby telephone pole with its cargo of long-distance messages. This evening the road is empty, yet he takes care to stay on one side of it. He can't predict when a car or pick-up truck might swerve down the hill, its driver foolhardy or drunk, forcing another vehicle to head for the ditch or a pedestrian to dive for his life. Though the speed limit is modest, there are guys who take pleasure in defying the rules. Breaking the limit is a macho game and, after all, a young man's car is his proof of virility. To lack a driver's licence is to be profoundly isolated—as isolated, indeed, as the young Indian appears to be. Lethbridge is a white man's town, and the nearest reserve is a long, long walk away.

The road, the telephone lines and the high tension wires connect the city with the river valley and the dry plateau beyond. Within the young man's lifetime, elegant homes have followed a small university to the far side of the valley. Not many natives ever go to university, or live in elegant homes—not as we define "elegant", anyway. Tonight's first stars will soon be in evidence on both sides of the river; the street lights are shining already. Further down the Oldman valley, there are no streets and few electric lights. Nor will there ever be, for much of the valley will shortly be lost under water collected by a costly, wasteful, probably unnecessary dam. Archaeologists of the future seeking to understand the patterns of land use in the area will have to don diving gear.

It's unlikely that the Indian is thinking about such matters. His broad, earth-coloured face lies in deep shadow. Try your hardest, and you still won't be able to make out many details of the man's appearance. Is he frowning with effort, is he trying to smile, is he keeping his face expressionless? Onto his tall frame, you can project whatever qualities of pain and nobility, of loneliness or mere futility, you believe should be seen there.

For the Indian is walking on crutches, and he's walking towards you. His crutches rest at the precise angle of the railway bridge's girders. High above the knee, his left leg has been amputated. He is standing on the toes of his only foot.

Not all of these photographs could or should be read like a drama. The full stories they tell can't be put into words. The meaning of the pictures begins and ends with their appearance: with the creased lines in a face, with the alignment of bales in a field, with the specific gesture made by a hand or hoof. These are pictures that invite attention, not judgement. Nobody in the photographs needs our approval.

Nobody is holding a camera, either. On the whole, westerners don't see themselves or their home region as especially photogenic—the colourful pictures on their living-room walls are more likely to show Peggy's Cove, Old Faithful, the Grand Canyon or some other natural wonder from outside the prairies. The rural west is an unglamorous land. Glamour, like women's fashion, is conceived of as something that happens elsewhere, reaching the prairies only late and secondhand.

In contrast to Parisians or New Yorkers or the inhabitants of almost every outcrop in the Aegean Sea, westerners are not accustomed to being photographed by strangers. Lacking a certain brand of self-importance, they may react with bemusement to the idea that their faces and homes are worth recording on somebody else's film. I was once sent a postcard of a grandiose prairie sunset; to my surprise, the caption described the capacity of an alfalfa-processing factory that was barely visible on the orange horizon. A picture-taking in the rural west is likely to be a moment of high ceremony: a wedding or a graduation, the christening of a child or the reunion of children who have grown up and gone. Such a picture gives the scattered components of a family a permanent image of something they desire to remember.

Another type of prairie ceremony occurs at chuckwagon races. The pictures in this book focus not just on the sweat, dust and danger of the actual races, but also on the expressions of the watching crowd and on all the small rituals that the wagon drivers create among themselves. The photographs capture the stillness before and after the speed. They invite us, too, to reflect on the survival of chuckwagon races in a high-tech age. Many of these spectators surely use satellite dishes, microwave ovens and personal computers in their homes. The future is hurling itself upon us; what point can there be in chuckwagons?

The point lies, perhaps, in their sheer endurance as an event still able to pull a western crowd, against all the competing attractions of electronic entertainment. People of all ages and both sexes gather at chuckwagon races, as they do at rodeos and fairs throughout the prairies. What they find there is the chance to act as a community. The races puncture the isolation that prairie space imposes. They provide an opportunity for fun—the fun of gossipping, of running into friends and running up against strangers, of eating and drinking outdoors, of flirting and joketelling and a hundred other activities. The fun, in short, of relaxing together.

Chuckwagon races are intimately tied to the history of western settlement, and to the notion that many prairie-dwellers have of their common identity. It's true that a few spectators might draw proud conclusions about the progress of society: "Is it only a century since people had to do their travelling in that kind of outfit?" More often, they're happy to contemplate, with pride and a dose of wistfulness, an image of their society's beginnings. Success in a chuckwagon race means the prompt, confident collaboration of a rider with his horses; it also implies a shrewd tactical judgement about the speed and strategy of fellow horsemen. Chuckwagons are valued as an indigenous contraption; a link to the great-grandfathers; a symbol, even, of some collective difference from people down east. Although our own travelling is faster and not quite so bumpy as it was a century ago, one of the commonest names for motels anywhere in the west is still "Pioneer".

Even today, there are ranchers who find a horse more efficient for many of their purposes than the most expensive machine. And despite its use of such unromantic devices as feedlots, abattoirs and artificial insemination units, western ranching retains a mythic quality. Some of the photographs in this book recall the ancient connection between human beings and animals, an intimacy older than Gilgamesh or Homer. The horses captured on film, like the people and even the cattle, are at home on their vast land. They belong. No doubt this is one of the reasons why these photographs can arouse such a strong sense of yearning.

North American cowboys have long been a part of world mythology. Seen from a distance, their days and nights have a clean simplicity free from the complications of urban life; free, as well, from the brutalities of history. Indeed, the west can offer enchanting images of escape. The tension in these photographs arises partly from an unresolved battle between romance and realism, between the dreamed-of west and the west's hard facts. For every image of a gentle twilight or a calm, well-cultivated farm, there's a counterpart that shows violent light, atrocious weather or somebody's abandoned home. These scenes of desolation are, unfortunately, true to the recent history of the rural west.

One task of photography should be to remind us of what's happening now—to help us remember the present as well as the past. (Just think about what's implied by the common phrase, "a fresh view".) There are always things we'd prefer to forget; and a photograph can get in the way of our all-too-convenient forgetfulness. Photographs can show us that what we think we recall about the west—and what the mass media choose to show us of the west—are not the whole story. If we look at the photographs with care, that is. For it's easy to see little in these pictures except the poignancy of defeat; easy to regard the images of old men and decaying farms with an urbane, regretful sigh.

Better to resist such attitudes. Better to find evidence here not only of what is past and passing, but also of what may be to come. Take a look, for example, at the photograph of about ten young Blackfeet at the Eden Valley powwow in Alberta. Seated in a circle, shouting or singing, they look as though they're addressing the central drum. It's the drum, not the photographer, that holds their rapt gaze. There is nothing traditional about their setting, nor about the chairs they're balancing on, nor about their clothes. And surely the participants in a Blackfoot powwow are "supposed" to sport robes and leggings, maybe even a feathered headdress? These men and boys are dressed like any other westerners, in caps and jeans and T-shirts. A visitor in search of the picturesque would find the Eden Valley scene a bitter disappointment: it's hard to be elegiac about a loud boy with a number 14 on his orange shirt.

It's also *wrong* to be elegiac—patronizing, and condescending, and inaccurate. What this photograph triumphantly demonstrates is the survival of Indian tradition, not its weakening from the pure and legendary past. The clothes and the setting are incidental to the vibrant force of a ritual that's being conducted for Indian purposes, not for the benefit of visitors. The drumming engages the entire attention, physical and mental, of the drummers. As they approach another century, the beat goes on. Nobody in the picture looks as though he belongs to a defeated people, a target for our sympathy. Nobody is staring, embarrassed, into the lens. Nobody is asking the photographer to immortalize the scene; but nobody is stopping him, either. He has a job to do, and so do they.

Look, too, at the picture of an old woman walking away from a domed Ukrainian church in southern Manitoba. At first glance, she presents a sad spectacle—hunched over, dressed too warmly for the spring or summer day, an ailing widow in a youthful country who clings to the patterned scarves and liturgy of her remote homeland. As she steps along the cracked, overgrown sidewalk, the camera tricks her into appearing one-legged. One way or another, she's on her way out. But stop: the photograph is not nearly as sentimental as that first impression. For the old woman is part of a community; other, younger members of it are visible on the sidewalk and the church steps behind her. The shape of their bright building expresses triumph, not misery. This woman is also well aware of her immediate surroundings and the day's possible weathers—remember the black umbrella she marshals with her left hand. Remember her face, too. Nothing in it asks for pity. Nothing in it calls to the photographer, "Help me!"

We can even think of these two pictures as forming part of a celebration. For all its faults, the rural west is a region where chuckwagon races, powwows and Ukrainian eucharists continue to thrive. Its diversity of cultures and landscapes is impressive; its appearance often defies the expectations of outsiders. And if the west invites nostalgia, it also resists that emotion. It's too untidy, too bloody-minded and occasionally too ugly to make nostalgia easy.

The people pictured here are perhaps baffled by fate, but I don't read despair on their faces. Caught in the west's unflinching light, they look proud to be who they are and to live where they do. Their battered dignity, their resilience, their refusal to accept the status of victim all conspire against nostalgia. Nobody in this book is humble in the face of the camera.

Yet the troubling facts remain, somewhere beyond the margins of the picture. The rural west is losing population; the land is increasingly depleted and eroded; the family farm is in danger of dying out. Thanks to the natural force of drought—combined with manmade forces of debt, greed, environmental wastage and political cynicism—a good part of a vast area is well on its way to becoming a ghostland. Westerners have always lived in Next Year Country, and it's still their common home. But on the bountiful, windswept prairies, there are fewer and fewer people left to hope.

The beauty in these photographs needs no justification. That beauty extends far beyond wild horses, rolling hills and the remorseless sky. It includes some human emotions too: tenacity, stubbornness and a shy tenderness that can blossom into anger.

106

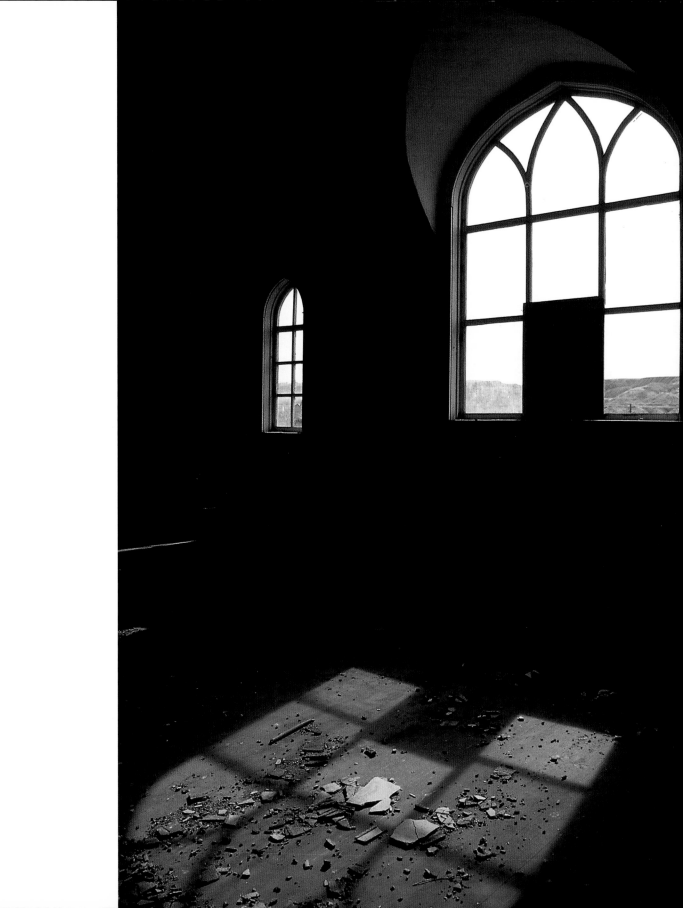

You leave the Chinese restaurant, finally. Beside the cash desk hangs an Oriental fan, embellished by a pair of dried poinsettias, and a collecting box for the Royal Canadian Legion. It's late in the afternoon, and the sun throws a long, diagonal shadow over the streets. The driver's seat and the steering wheel are hot to the touch. As you drive slowly through the grid of roads, you notice that one of the streets has the unlikely name of Pacific Avenue.

Most of the homes look trim, most of the lawns well watered. Sprinklers stand in front of windowpanes. On impulse, you choose an old, little-used highway and begin a circuitous trip back to the city. At the edge of town is a big disused hall with a painted rainbow high above the bolted doors and a small anthology of political posters smeared on the walls. A dog at the first farm bounds to the edge of the road, barking exuberantly; in the mirror you see it trotting back home, its tail still busy. The fields are glowing in the light.

The road leads down into a glacial valley, its floor occupied by a narrow lake. Berry bushes slither down the slopes of the valley, and a scent of wild sage pours in through the car windows. At the water's edge there's a rusting beachfront playground, even though there's not much of a beach. Beyond it, a mile or more from the nearest house, stands an abandoned car. Its back wheels rest on the brown shore, but its front wheels are immersed in water. None of its windows has been broken, and the red paintwork is still bright. The licence plate dates from last year.

Puzzled, wondering, you drive on. The road finds the far side of the valley and climbs back onto the plain. Almost immediately, the lake is lost to view. A rising wind sends dust clouds through the air, forcing you to roll up the window. In one section of the sky, clouds form a great arc. That's when you notice, off in the distance, a bluff of evergreen trees.

They turn out to be spruces, marking a graveyard apparently in the middle of nowhere. Probably it's the cemetery of the next town along the road; a dark grain elevator is looming up ahead. Intrigued by the trees, you stop the car and walk through a memorial gate. Frisky lambs are carved on the tombstones of a clutch of small children, dead from influenza after the First World War. The adult graves that don't have crosses on top are pointing into the sky like joined hands at prayer. They've garnered some withered flowers beneath the oddly life-doubting phrases: *Thy Rest Is Won; Passed By Here; With Christ Which Is Far Better*.

It's strange that you didn't hear the approaching car of the other visitor. He's standing at the entrance to the graveyard now, wearing jeans and cowboy boots, a check shirt and a denim jacket. When he takes off his cap to wipe his brow, you notice that his cropped hair is silvery. He walks towards you slowly and heavily, like a man accustomed to the rhythms of the earth. A small, elusive bird is singing from the top of a spruce.

"Afternoon," you say as you pass.

"Afternoon," he replies. You can see the grey stubble on his creased jaw and the humour lines around his mouth. One of his cheeks is scarred. His eyes, narrowed from years of assessing the sun, the wind and the faint prospect of rain, burn with a cool, indomitable fire. This is nobody, you think to yourself, who would give up without a fight. You saw how broad his hands and shoulders were.

But when you turn around, he's gone.

List of Plates

Ottmar Bierwagen was born in West Germany and came to Canada as a boy. He studied at Sheridan College and Trent University (Peterborough), and has taught photojournalism in Canada and the United States. He worked as Director of Photography for the *Winnipeg Free Press* and as a Picture Editor for the *Toronto Star,* and has won numerous photojournalism awards including Ontario Newsphotographer of the Year (1979 and 1980) and Magazine Photographer of the Year (1985). He uses exclusively Kodak's Kodachrome 64 transparency film.

Ottmar Bierwagen is currently a freelance photographer for *Equinox, Canadian Living,* and *National Geographic,* and he maintains an active business in corporate/industrial photography. His works have been published in *Calgary, Heart of the West; A Day in the Life of Canada; Share the Flame; the XV Olympic Winter Games,* and, for Douglas & McIntyre, *Canada: The Great Lone Land.*

Mark Abley was born in England in 1955. From age six to twenty he lived in Lethbridge and Saskatoon. After winning a Bachelor of Arts degree from the University of Saskatchewan, he went to Oxford on a Rhodes scholarship and received his Master of Arts degree in English Language and Literature. He and his wife and daughter live in Montreal.

Mark Abley is a feature writer at the Montreal *Gazette* and a contributing editor of *Saturday Night.* He has contributed regularly to *Maclean's,* CBC Radio's "Ideas" and *The Times Literary Supplement.* He is the author of a book of poems, BLUE SAND, BLUE MOON, published by Cormorant Books (1988). In 1986, Douglas & McIntyre published his book, *Beyond Forget: Rediscovering the Prairies.*